Fire

Written by
Jill Atkins

Fire has a lot of uses, so it is very handy!

In fact, people have used fire for thousands of years for lighting, heating and cooking.

How do we use fire now?

We use it now in the same ways that we did long ago.

We can use fire for lighting a dark place, or to keep us snug if we sit by the fire at home.

In winter it is good to roast chestnuts on the fire.

We can cook dinner on a gas stove.

The flame will be hot, so we can fry eggs or bake a pie.

We can cook outside too, on a barbecue or a camp fire.

Some people cook chicken. Other people cook fish or burgers.

We can smoke fish or meat too.

When the food is done, it will taste good!

Fire has many other uses.

Steam trains have very hot coal fires to make the steam that makes the trains go.

Blacksmiths have fires of coal or charcoal to heat metal.

When the metal is red hot it is a bit soft, so the blacksmith can hammer it into shape. She can make tools, gates, fences and other things.

Some people make pots. They are called potters.

They use clay to make pots on a wheel, or with their hands.

Then, when the pots are dry, the potter lights the **kiln**, which has a very hot fire inside. The potter fires the pottery in the kiln.

Bricks are made this way too.

Do you like to see sparks and patterns of fire in the sky?

These people are at a bonfire party. They are enjoying looking up into the dark night sky!

Danger!

Fire can be used in so many ways, but it can be a danger too!

So we must stay safe, so that we do not get hurt!

In some places where there are forests,
the weather can get very hot and dry.
If there is no rain, there might be a forest fire.

The forest fire might spread quickly.

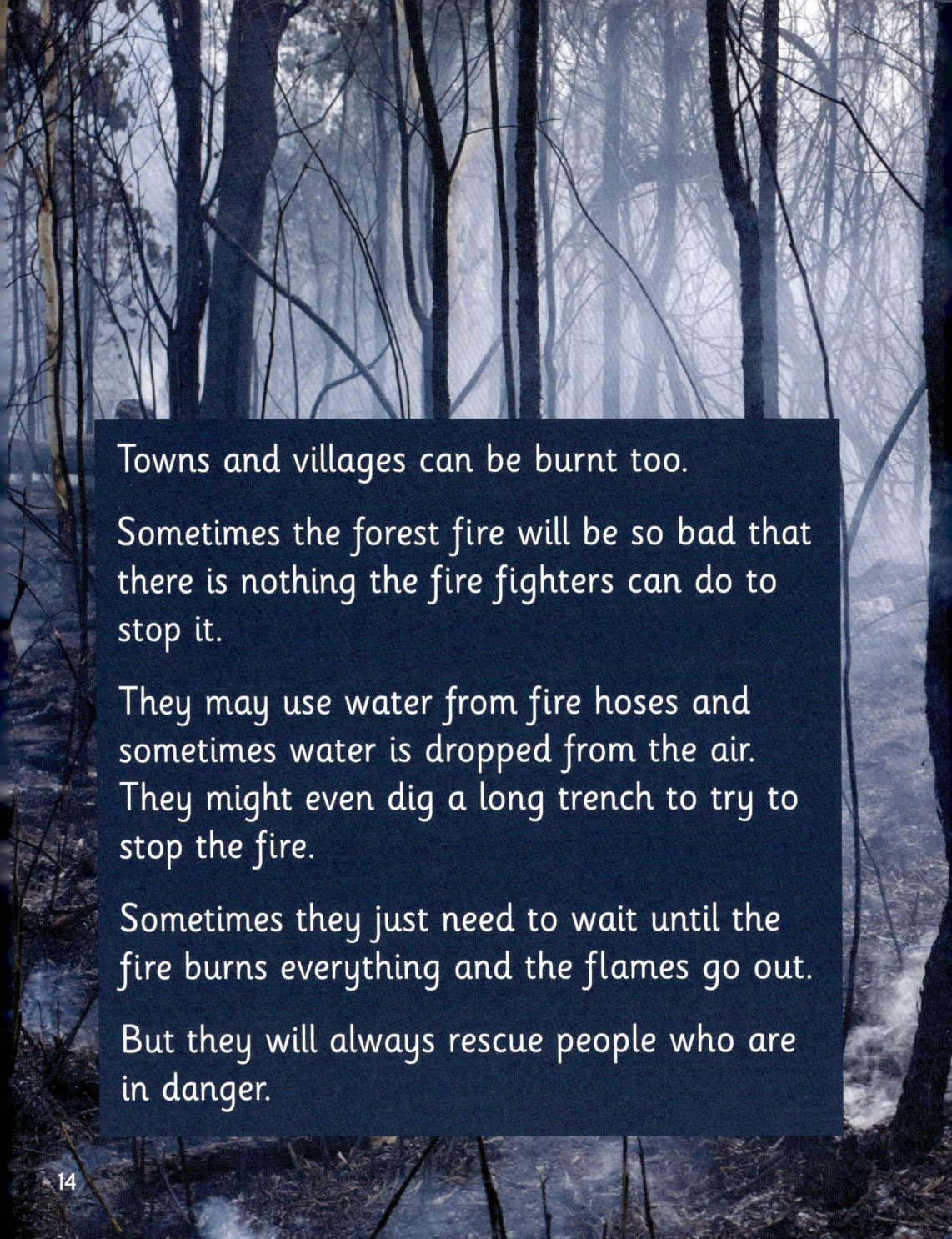

Towns and villages can be burnt too.

Sometimes the forest fire will be so bad that there is nothing the fire fighters can do to stop it.

They may use water from fire hoses and sometimes water is dropped from the air. They might even dig a long trench to try to stop the fire.

Sometimes they just need to wait until the fire burns everything and the flames go out.

But they will always rescue people who are in danger.

Fire fighters getting ready to fight a forest fire

As long as we keep safe, fire is a good thing for us to use!